11/17

A+
books

How to Be a
GOOD
CITIZEN

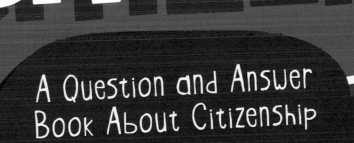

A Question and Answer
Book About Citizenship

by Emily James

CAPSTONE PRESS
a capstone imprint

Members of a community are called citizens.

Being a good citizen means working to make your community a better place.

It also means helping to make
the world a better place.

There are lots of ways to be a good citizen.

Marco hears his friend being bullied.

How can Marco be a good citizen?

Marco finds an adult to help.
He is being a good citizen.

**How can you help someone
who is being bullied?**

Noah thinks the lake near his home needs to be cleaner.

How could Noah be a good citizen?

Noah and his sister learn about the environment and find ways to help.

Noah is being a good citizen.

How could you help the environment?

Lucy goes to the library.
She checks out two new books.

How can Lucy be a good citizen?

Lucy takes good care of the books. She is respecting the library's property. She is also being a good citizen.

How can you show respect for someone else's things?

A new family moved into Kate's neighborhood.

What can Kate do to be a good citizen?

Kate visits the family to say hello.
She is welcoming new people to her
community. She is also being a good citizen.

**How could you
help someone
new feel
welcome?**

Emma goes outside to play.

She sees her neighbor carrying her garbage.

How can Emma be a good citizen?

Emma helps her neighbor take the trash bag to the street. Being a good citizen means being a good neighbor.

How can you be a good neighbor?

Olivia spots some trash on the ground.

How can Olivia be a good citizen?

Olivia picks up the trash. She puts it in the trash can. Good citizens don't litter. They help keep the community clean.

What can you do to keep your community clean?

Election day is coming up.
People need to know about
the candidates.

How can Colin be a good citizen?

Colin helps his mom hand out flyers. He hopes adults will vote. Good citizens vote in elections.

What can you do to help at election time?

Mrs. Jones is a history teacher.

How does she help to make her students good citizens?

Mrs. Jones teaches her students about their country. Being a good citizen means knowing your country's history.

What do you know about your country's history?

Nina has a lot of toys. She doesn't have time to play with them all.

How can Nina be a good citizen?

Nina donates some of her toys.
Good citizens donate to charity.

What are some other things you could donate?

DONATE

Omar wants to ask his teacher a question.

He knows the rule is to raise his hand.

What should Omar do to be a good citizen?

Omar raises his hand before speaking.
Good citizens follow rules.

What are some important rules that you follow?

Maria and Levi want to make their neighborhood look nice.

What can they do to be good citizens?

Maria and Levi plant flowers.

Good citizens make the
world a better place.

**What can you do to make
the world a better place?**

Gunner has ideas to improve his school.

What can Gunner do to be a good citizen?

Gunner can run for class president.
Good citizens are leaders.

Vote for Gunner!!! More Free Writing Time

In what ways can you be a leader?

Ethan knows some people in his community are in need.

How can Ethan be a good citizen?

28

Ethan volunteers to help pack food for the homeless. Good citizens help those in need.

How can you help someone in need?

Glossary

candidate—a person who runs for office, such as president

charity—a group that raises money or collects goods to help people in need

citizen—a member of a country, state, or community who has the right to live there

donate—to give something as a gift to a charity or cause

election—the process of choosing someone or deciding something by voting

environment—all of the trees, plants, water, and dirt

volunteer—to offer to do something without pay

Internet Sites

Use FactHound to find Internet sites related to this book:

Visit *www.facthound.com*

Just type in 9781515771951 and go.

Read More

Higgins, Melissa. *I Am a Good Citizen*. I Don't Bully! North Mankato, Minn.: Capstone Press, 2014.

Ponto, Joanna. *Being a Good Citizen*. All About Character. New York: Enslow Publishing, 2016.

Zuchora-Walske, Christine. *How Can I Be a Good Digital Citizen?* Lightning Bolt Books: Our Digital World. Minneapolis: Lerner Publishing Group, 2016.

Critical Thinking Questions

1. How is Marco a good citizen when he hears his friend being bullied?

2. Volunteering is one way you can be a good citizen. What does it mean to volunteer? Hint: Use your glossary for help!

3. Can you think of a time you were a good citizen? What did you do?

Index

A+ Books are published by Capstone Press,
1710 Roe Crest Drive, North Mankato, Minnesota 56003
www.mycapstone.com

Library of Congress Cataloging-in-Publication Data
Cataloging-in-publication information is on file with the Library of Congress.

ISBN: 978-1-5157-7195-1 (library binding)
ISBN: 978-1-5157-7203-3 (eBook PDF)

Editorial Credits
Jaclyn Jaycox, editor; Heidi Thompson, designer; Jo Miller, media researcher;
Laura Manthe, production specialist; Marcy Morin, scheduler

Photo Credits
All photographs by Capstone Studio/Karon Dubke. except:
Shutterstock: Alinute Silzeviciute, 24, 25, Lopolo, 4, 5, Poznukhov
Yurly, 6, 7, RoyStudioEU throughout, (background texture).

Printed in the United States of America.
010374F17